MW01240903

This journal belongs to:

Made in the USA
Middletown, DE
07 August 2022

70782238R00064